MW00885615

Sort the animals correctly.

Jellyfish	Whale	Squid	Cockroach	Manatee	Dolphin
Sea horse	Shark	Butterfly	Parrot	Hummingbird	Bat
Starfish	Earthworm	Snail	Octopus		

Invertebrates	Vertebrates

Notes:

_____

_____

OLYMPIAD TESTER

Name: _____

Date: _____

Fill in the blanks with the words given in the box to complete the passage on "CAMOUFLAGE".

boas	scampering	brown	grassy	survival
leaf	predators	green	pattern	blending
Prey	squirrel	trees	colors	marks
pythons	savanna	camouflage	African	trunks
spots				

In nature, _____ and prey seem to play a game of hide and seek. _____ need to hide, so predators do not find them and eat them. Predators need to hide too, so smaller prey cannot see them approaching. Some animals have special _____ or _____ on their bodies that help them hide among _____, rocks, and grass. This blending is called _____.

The earth tone colors of deer and squirrels help them hide from predators among the browns of trees, bushes and soil. A brown _____ can be difficult to see when it is _____ among brown autumn leaves. A brown deer can be overlooked when it is hiding between tree _____. The deer and squirrel's special coloring help them hide from predators.

_____ lions have a tan body coloring. However, lions use it not to hide from predators, but to hide in _____ grasses while watching for prey. A lion can sneak up on prey without being seen more easily by _____ into the _____ environment.

Another popular animal camouflage color is green. The green tree frogs of Australia blend in and hide from predators better because of their color. Green tree _____ and emerald _____, meanwhile, are more like lions, using their green color to blend in. When a likely meal (a rodent, bird or lizard) comes along these snakes strike quickly, catching the prey.

The praying mantis takes things a step further. While its _____ to _____ color helps it blend in with vegetation, the mantis also mimics the shape of a stem or _____. The mantis uses these camouflage methods both to hide from predators like birds, frogs, snakes, spiders and bats, and to await prey such as insects (including other mantises!), spiders, hummingbirds, and small frogs and mice.

Just as important as color camouflage and mimicry is _____ camouflage.

Tiger stripes and leopard and jaguar _____ are all patterns which help these cats hide among the plants and shadows when they search for prey.

In nature, hide-and-seek is a game of life and death. Pattern and color camouflage, and mimicry, can give predatorsand prey a _____ advantage.

Write at least 3 more examples of camouflage:

....

....

....

4

Write the characteristics of birds, fish, mammals, reptiles, and amphibians in this table

	Birds	Fish	Mammals	Reptiles	Amphibians
Covering What type of body covering do animals in this group have? (ex: scales)					
Blood Are animals in this group warm-blooded or coldblooded?					
Breathing Do the animals in this group breathe air (lungs) or water (gills)?					
Birth Do the young hatch from eggs or are they born alive?			)		
Milk Do the young drink milk from their mother?					
Backbone Do animals in this group have a skeleton with a backbone?					

5

 OLYMPIAD
TESTER

05ANIMALS | WS 04

Name: _____

Date: _____

Fill in the blanks with the words given in the box to complete the passage on "adaptations of an arctic fox ".

lemming	hibernate	mammal	scarf	smell
tunnels	rocks	paws	hunter	camouflage
bears	adapted	habitat	northern	fluffy
burrows	fat	omnivores	energy	

A fascinating hunter makes its home in the Arctic tundra. The _____ white _____ is known to leap high in the air before pouncing on the burrow of its suspected prey. After a few seconds of furious digging, the small _____ emerges from the snow-covered ground with a tasty snack, a _____. What animal uses such acrobatic hunting techniques? The arctic fox.

Arctic foxes live in all regions of the _____ Arctic. You might be surprised to learn that arctic foxes don't _____, even though their _____ is very cold. They live in underground _____ and are active throughout the year. These foxes are amazingly _____ for their habitat. Thick multilayered fur keeps them extra warm. In winter, this coat is white (or occasionally blue-gray). This provides _____ in the snow and ice.

In summer, the coat turns a brown-gray, helping the foxes blend in with _____ and small Arctic tundra plants. Arctic foxes have a big fluffy tail. This tail makes a great _____. Meanwhile, their furry paws, small ears, and short muzzle helps prevent heat loss. The fur on the bottom of their _____ keeps them from slipping when they run across ice.

As winter approaches, Arctic foxes increase their body _____ by eating as much as they can. This fat provides extra insulation and _____. What do arctic foxes eat? Since these animals are _____, they eat other animals (lemmings, hares, small birds, fish, as well as eggs) and plants (berries and seaweed). When food is scarce, they eat the scraps left behind by polar _____ and wolves. Arctic foxes can find prey above ground or beneaththe snow because of their excellent senses of hearing and _____.

Arctic foxes usually mate for life. The mother gives birth to five, ten, or even more pups. Both parents raise the pups in underground dens that often include a network of many _____.

Name: _____

Date: _____

Read the passage below and answer the questions.

What mammal lives only in the Americas, looks a little like a monster-sized pillbug, and wears a coat of armor on its back, head, legs, and tail?

An armadillo, of course.

What is an armadillo's armor like? The armadillo's armor is made up of plates of skin-covered bone. Between these bony sections are flexible bands of skin. Hair grows through the skin on these bands and also on the animal's sides and much softer belly. How many bands an armadillo has depends upon the species.

Where do armadillos live? Wild armadillos live in the grasslands, forests, and deserts of North and South America. One species, the nine-banded armadillo, has extended its range as far north as the United States. They can be found in several states, including Texas, Florida, Georgia, and the Carolinas. Most other species live in South America, with some also in Central America and Mexico.

How big are they? The smallest armadillo, the pink fairy armadillo, is only six inches long. Meanwhile, the giant armadillo can be five feet long and weigh up to 100 pounds. The nine-branded variety that is found in the United States can grow up to two feet long and weigh up to 22 pounds.

Can they roll up in a ball to protect themselves from predators? While the animal's armor provides some protection, only the small three-banded armadillo can roll into a complete ball. Other species escape predators like wild cats and birds of prey by racing into thorny bushes or by burrowing into the ground with their sharp claws. In fact, most armadillos sleep in the warmth of an underground burrow.

What do armadillos eat? Their main diet consists of insects. Using their nose for smelling and their claws for digging, armadillos find beetles, ants and termites and pull them into their mouths with their worm-like tongues. Armadillos also eat plants, fruit, eggs, and small animals, both alive and dead.

What time of day does an armadillo search for food? Well, that depends on the season. Armadillos don't do well in cold weather, so in winter they come out more during the warmth of day. In summer they become more nocturnal, coming out during the night or at dusk or dawn.

Do armadillos swim? You'd think swimming with a suit of armor would be hard.

However, by gulping air into their digestive tract armadillos are able to stay afloat as they paddle. Armadillos can also go underwater and walk along a stream bottom for up to six minutes.

Do armadillos live in groups? Armadillos tend to be solitary. However, when it's cold they do sometimes group together.

What are baby armadillos like? At birth an armadillo's armor is soft and leathery. It hardens as the animal grows. Armadillo mothers give birth to differing numbers of young depending upon the species. The nine-banded armadillo always has four identical babies, either four brothers or four sisters.

Are armadillos endangered? The nine-banded variety is not endangered, and their numbers are growing. Most other armadillo varieties are decreasing in number. They've lost habitat to farms and other human settlements. Also, armadillos are often hit by cars while crossing roads. A few people even hunt them for food.

1. An armadillo's diet is mainly composed of _____

   ....

2. Can armadillos roll up in a ball to protect themselves from predators?

   ....

   ....

3. Name two natural predators of armadillos mentioned in the article

   ....

4. Are Armadillos an endangered species

   ....

5. An adult armadillo in the United States would probably measure about...

   ....

6. Is armadillo a reptile?

   ....

7. Are armadillos nocturnal?

   ....

8. How big is the group of armadillos?

Name: _____

Date: _____

Fill in the blanks with the words from the box to complete sentences.

feathers	Turtle	deaf	teeth	Dogs
eagle	Whiskers	echolocation	enemy	friend
fangs	smell	Whale	ears	Insects

1. Mosquitoes can find you by the _____ of your body

2. _____ have an extraordinary sense of smell

3. An _____ can spot it's prey from miles away

4. Dolphins and bats use _____ for movement

5. _____ help the tiger to move in dark and find it's prey

6. Birds do not have _____

7. A snake has two hollow teeth called _____

8. Snakes do not have external _____

9. Snake is a/an _____ of the farmer

10. Rat is a/an _____ of the farmer

11. Snakes are born _____. They can only feel vibrations and move with that.

12. _____ are the largest group of animals on Earth

13. _____ is a lung breathing aquatic animal

14. The butterfly has wings but no _____.

15. _____ is an aquatic animals that lays eggs on land only

Name: _____

Date: _____

Fill in the blanks with the words from the box to complete sentences.

tiny	dolphins	Vertebrates	vertebral column	octopus
insects	marine	moist skin	invertebrates	Reptiles

1. Invertebrates are animals that neither possess nor develop a

   _____

2. More than 90% of the animals are _____

3. _____ are the broad group of animals which are classified by the possession of a backbone or spinal column

4. The _____ is considered to be the smartest invertebrates

5. Mammals, Fish, Amphibians, Birds and _____ are all vertebrates

6. Spiders and _____ are invertebrates

7. Crabs, prawns, crayfish & lobsters are _____ vertebates

8. Invertebrates are normally _____ and slow moving animals

9. Though _____ and whales are not fish though they live in water and resemble them. They are mammals

10. Frogs breathe through their _____ when they are under water

Name: _____

Date: _____

Fill in the blanks with the words given in the box to complete the passage on "adaptations in grassland animals ".

environment	Structural	physical	habitats	Organisms
Behavioral	enemies	respond	water	

Adaptation occur in response to changes in the _____, lifestyle, or relationship to other organisms. _____ that are adapted to their _____ are able to secure food and _____, obtain spaces, cope with _____ conditions such as temperature, light, and heat, defend themselves from their natural _____, reproduce successfully, _____ to changes around them

There are different types of adaptations:

_____ Adaptations – These are special body parts of an organism that helps organisms to survive in its natural habitat. Example: skin colour, shape, etc.

Physiological Adaptations – These are mechanisms present in an organism that allow it to perform certain biochemical reactions to survive in its natural habitat. Example: ability to produce venom, ability to maintain a constant body temperature, etc.

_____ Adaptations – These are ways a particular organism behaves to survive in its natural habitat. Example: being active at night

12

Name: _____

Date: _____

Try to solve the crossword within 10 minutes.

Across

1. forests, grasslands, deserts, coastal and mountain regions
2. Respond to change
3. Have backbones
4. Do not have backbones
7. lakes, ponds, rivers and streams, wetlands, swamp, etc
8. oceans, intertidal zone, reefs, seabed
9. Another name for habitat
11. Fish and Reptiles have ___.
12. Amphibian breathe through this
14. Helps the arctic fox to hide in snow
15. Active at night

Down

5. Live on both land and water
6. natural phenomenon to disguise themselves
10. The movement of organisms in large numbers from one place to another place
13. A smart invertebrate

Name: _____

Date: _____

Do the correct matching.

1	LAND HABITAT -	- natural phenomenon to disguise themselves	A
2	ADAPTATION -	- Respond to change	B
3	VERTEBRATES -	- Helps the arctic fox to hide in snow	C
4	INVERTEBRATES -	- Live on both land and water	D
5	AMPHIBIANS -	- Have backbones	E
6	CAMOUFLAGE -	- Do not have backbones	F
7	FRESHWATER HABITAT -	- Active at night	G
8	MARINE HABITAT -	- Fish and Reptiles have ___.	H
9	BIOME -	- forests, grasslands, deserts, coastal and mountain regions	I
10	MIGRAION -	- oceans, intertidal zone, reefs, seabed	J
11	SCALES -	- Amphibian breathe through this	K
12	MOIST SKIN -	- Another name for habitat	L
13	Octopus -	- A smart invertebrate	M
14	WHITE FUR -	- The movement of organisms in large numbers from one place to another place	N
15	NOCTURNAL -	- lakes, ponds, rivers and streams, wetlands, swamp, etc	O

Name: _____

Date: _____

Search for the words in the puzzle. Words are placed in all directions (including reverse) and tightly interweaved.

S	N	A	I	B	I	H	P	M	A	X	P	O	W	R	S
E	C	L	D	N	O	I	F	D	R	C	O	I	U	B	E
T	W	A	M	A	R	I	N	E	H	A	B	I	T	A	T
A	O	N	L	I	P	D	T	M	Q	O	M	G	C	P	A
R	U	D	T	E	Z	T	E	R	G	X	Y	B	M	M	R
B	Z	H	Q	J	S	V	A	Y	D	K	I	M	V	N	B
E	S	A	E	Z	N	F	L	T	H	L	Q	W	P	C	E
T	I	B	M	I	G	R	A	T	I	O	N	I	K	S	T
R	M	I	O	W	Z	K	N	P	M	O	I	S	T	Y	R
E	M	T	P	H	T	S	R	J	O	A	N	U	L	V	E
V	H	A	D	I	Y	F	U	C	D	Y	C	U	C	W	V
N	J	T	I	T	Q	G	T	I	B	U	N	Q	D	W	H
I	U	N	J	E	O	O	C	I	Y	A	R	Q	R	M	V
N	G	B	N	F	P	Q	O	S	P	O	E	C	V	I	L
E	Z	Q	D	U	H	M	N	U	S	I	J	I	E	U	J
W	H	M	S	R	E	G	A	L	F	U	O	M	A	C	F

LAND HABITAT	ADAPTATION	VERTEBRATES	INVERTEBRATES	AMPHIBIANS	CAMOUFLAGE
MARINE HABITAT	BIOME	MIGRATION	SCALES	MOIST	SKIN
Octopus	WHITE FUR	NOCTURNAL			

Name: _____

Date: _____

Unscramble the words

1. **htbaaandlt i**   L _ _ _   _ _ _ _   A T

2. **ta adaption**   A _ A P _ _ _ _ _ _

3. **bet traverse**   V _ R _ _ _ R _ _ _ _

4. **vie terebrants**   _ _ _ E _ _ _ _ R _ T _ _

5. **bi pashmina**   A M _ _ _ _ I _ _ _

6. **ef glaucoma**   _ A _ _ _ _ L _ G _

7. **a raibihenmatt**   M A _ _ _ _   _ A _ _ _ T

8. **be moi**   B _ _ _ _

9. **it roaming**   _ _ _ _ _ T I _ _

10. **el sacs**   _ _ A L _ _

11. **moits**   _ _ I _ _

12. **kins**   _ _ _ N

13. **u coopts**   O _ _ _ p _ _

14. **if wuther**   _ _ I _ _   _ _ R

15. **no truncal**   _ _ _ _ _ _ N A _

Name: _____

Date: _____

Decode the cryptogram to reveal two amazing animals facts.

A	B	C	D	E	F	G	H	I	J	K	L	M	N	O	P	Q	R	S	T	U	V	W	X	Y	Z
		71	80																87		72		73		

T _ _   _ _ _ _ _ _ _ _   T   _ _ _ _ _   _ _   T _ _
87 85 68   81 89 74 75 75 68 81 87   81 82 74 76 68   70 82   87 85 68

W _ _ D   _ _   T _ _   T _ _ _ _ D
72 69 86 75 80   70 81   87 85 68   87 85 86 68 74 80

_ _ _ _ _ ,   _ _ _ _ D   _ _   T _ _   W _ _ T
81 82 74 76 68   83 69 90 82 80   70 82   87 85 68   72 68 81 87

_ _ D _ _ _ .   W _ _ _   _ T   _ _
70 82 80 70 68 81   72 85 68 82   70 87   70 81

_ _ _ _ - _ _ _ W _   _ T   _ _   _ _ _ _ T
83 90 75 75   78 86 69 72 82   70 87   70 81   74 67 69 90 87

T _ _ _ _   _ _ C _ _ _   _ _ _ _ .
87 85 86 68 68   70 82 71 85 68 81   75 69 82 78

_ _ _ _ _ _ _ _ _   T _ T _ _ _ _ _ _   _ _ _
78 74 75 74 84 74 78 69 81   87 69 86 87 69 70 81 68 81   74 86 68

_ _ _ _   _ _   T _ _   T _ _   _ _ D _ T
81 69 89 68   69 83   87 85 68   87 85 68   69 75 80 68 81 87

_ _ _ _ _ _   _ _ _ _ _ _ _   _ _   _ _ _ T _ .
75 70 88 70 82 78   74 82 70 89 74 75 81   69 82   68 74 86 87 85

_ _ _   T _ _ T _ _ _ _ _   _ _   _ _ _ W _ T _
69 82 68   87 69 86 87 69 70 81 68   70 81   76 82 69 72 82   87 69

_ _   _ _ _ _   _ _ _ D _ _ D   _ _ D   _ _ _ T Y
67 68   69 88 68 86   85 90 82 80 86 68 80   74 82 80   83 70 83 87 73

Y _ _ _ _   _ _ D .
73 68 74 86 81   69 75 80

18

 OLYMPIAD TESTER

05ANIMALS | WS 14

Name: _____

Date: _____

Unscramble the sentences to reveal few amazing animal facts.

1. _____ _____ _____ _____ ____
   _____ _____ _____ _____
   ___ _____ _____ _____ _____ _____

   heaviest / of / type / The / snake / grow to over / green / is the /
   anaconda. / can / pounds. / 300 / in the world / It

2. __ _____ _____ _____ _____
   _____ ___ _____

   _____

   threatened. / blood / can / A / squirt / horned / when / it feels / out of
   its / lizard / eyes

3. _____ _____ _____ ____ _____
   _____ ___ _____ ____
   _____ _____ _____ _____
   _____ _____ _____ _____

   _____

   largest / of / eat / It / The / and / dragon / even / species / Komodo
   / deer, / to / lizard / on / goats, / has been known / horses! / birds, /
   monkeys, / Earth. / is the

4. _____ _____ _____ _____ _____
   _____ _____ _____

   species / of / through / can / their / Some / eyelids. / snakes / see

www.olympiadtester.com   18

5. _____ _____ _____ ___ _____ _____ _____

____ _____ _____ _____ _____

it. / turtle / a / bones / shell / The / 60 / inside / has / of / over / of

OLYMPIAD TESTER

Unscramble the sentences to reveal few amazing animal facts.

1. _____ _____ _____ _____ _____

   _____ _____

   live / Antarctica. / in / Turtles / except / every / continent

2. _____ _____ _____ _____

   _____

   eighty / teeth. / about / Alligators / have

3. _____ _____ _____ _____ _____

   _____ _____ _____ _____ _____

   _____ _____ _____ _____ _____ _____ ___

   _____ _____ _____ _____ _____

   _____

   and / beach / bury / up to / to / return / sea / and / at a time. / They / turtles / fifty / Female / lay / ocean. / eggs / sandy / eggs / the / their / on a / hundred

4. _____ ___ _____ _____ _____ _____

   ____ _____ _____ _____ _____

   a / lizard / can / it / its / When / new / one. / tail, / loses / grow / a

5. _____ _____ _____ _____ ____

   _____ _____ _____

   to / their / environment. / use / tongues / Snakes / smell / their

6.

_____ _____ _____ _____ _____ _____

_____ _____ _____ _____

_____ _____ _____ _____ _____

_____ _____ _____ _____ _____ _____

_____ _____ _____ _____ _____ _____

_____ _____ _____ _____

their / They / in / bodies / forest. / like / glide / lizards. / birds, / Southeast / In / there / can / tree / and / to / They / are / flying / from / fly / don't / exactly / flatten / though. / Asia, / actually / the / tree

Name: _____

Date: _____

Search for 20 INVERTEBRATES in the puzzle. They are placed in all directions (including reverse) and tightly interweaved.

E	W	C	E	N	T	I	P	E	D	E	P
Y	L	F	R	E	T	T	U	B	I	R	K
S	G	U	L	S	E	A	S	T	A	R	Z
H	S	P	O	N	G	E	T	W	N	R	K
O	C	T	O	P	U	S	N	U	I	P	C
N	C	O	C	K	R	O	A	C	H	P	O
E	T	S	R	E	D	I	P	S	C	R	R
Y	P	E	P	I	S	I	W	O	R	M	A
B	P	S	L	I	A	N	S	H	U	F	L
E	N	O	M	E	N	A	I	F	A	J	S
E	M	U	P	L	O	B	S	T	E	R	K
E	D	E	P	I	L	L	I	M	S	P	P

Spiders	Insects	Millipede	Centipede	Worm	Sea star
Sea urchin	Anemone	Corals	Snails	Slugs	Sponge
Honeybee	Crab	Prawn	Lobster	Octopus	Cockroach
Butterfly	Ant				

Name: _____

Date: _____

Fill in the blanks with the words given in the box to complete the passage on "scorpions".

vibrations	insects	caves	inches	pincers
nocturnal	feet	consumption	sight	hair-like
night	tail	dangerous	digestive	predators
dinosaurs	Antarctica	smallest	dangerous	eight
venomous				

If you've ever seen a scorpion, I doubt you would consider it a "cute and cuddly" creature. With its big claw-like _____ and its long, curled _____ and _____ stinger, a scorpion is definitely a scary sight. However, only around 30 of the nearly 2,000 species of scorpions have venom considered _____ to humans.

Like spiders and other arachnids, scorpions have _____ legs and eat meat. They live in deserts, grasslands, forests, and jungles. You can find scorpions on every continent except _____.

Scorpions are _____, or active during the _____. They often hide in dark, cool places like leaf litter, burrows, and _____. And, yes, they like dark corners in buildings and homes, too. Ancient relatives of scorpions lived before the _____. Some of these prehistoric scorpion-like creatures grew up to several _____ in length. Luckily, today's scorpions are a lot smaller. Most are less than three _____.

You might be surprised to learn that the _____ scorpions are often the most _____. Some examples of deadly scorpions are the Indian red scorpion, the Deathstalker of Africa and the Middle East, and the Arizona bark scorpion. Most large species, including the eight-inch African emperor scorpion, are much less dangerous.

Scorpions don't have a good sense of _____. But they do have sensory _____ structures on their legs and bodies. These structures are capable of feeling vibrations from nearby _____, including tarantulas, centipedes, lizards, owls, bats, shrews, and mice. They can also feel _____ from their prey, which include a variety of _____, centipedes, spiders, and sometimes, even other scorpions.

Sometimes a scorpion will use its stinger to overcome its prey. All species of scorpions have _____ juices that help soften the scorpion's food, allowing for easy _____.

Name: _____

Date: _____

Fill in the blanks with the words given in the box to complete the passage on "ADAPTATIONS".

habitat	withstand	survival	survive	animals
ocean	chameleon	burrowing	color	protection
food	migrate	Antarctica	fat	Grassland
Habitat	hump	reproduction	adaptation	Desert
predators	Tundra	evolution	dominating	climate

_____ is too hot while _____ is too cold for a man to live. But these are _____ for some _____. The property which helps these animals to live in these extreme conditions is called _____. Adaptation of animals differs from region to region and according to the _____.

_____ is the natural place where animals live. Different organisms prefer the distinct type of conditions and habitat. It may be as big as an _____ or as small as a lake. Some are aquatic while some are terrestrial animals or both. Different types of habitats found on earth are Water, Desert, Forest, _____, _____ and few more. Every animal is native to some region, some _____ from one region to another according to climate.

Adaptation of Animals

When life forms native to an area begin to face some changes in their environment or any threats, either they will die or will adapt for _____. Adaptations are approaches by animals or any organism to live or _____ in a specific condition. Every living being is adapted to its habitat. A variety of adaptations can be observed in animals which include behavioral, physiological, anatomical or morphological. The reason for adaptations may be competition for _____, weather or for _____. As per researchers and scientists, adaptation is the result of _____ over few generations.

Depending on the climate and habitat, animals may show adaptations like changes in _____ and thickness of skin or fur, shapes of body parts like nose, ears etc. Few types of adaptations are as follow:

Adaptations to extremes: Animals have behavioral and physiological adaptations to _____ the harsh conditions like scarcity of water or oxygen, cold, toxic and corrosive chemicals. For example, _____ on a camel for _____ storage etc.

Psychological adaptations: Few animals have learning skills like using tools, swimming, emotional behavior like a human. They learn by observation, trials; some mimic others like a _____. E.g. Vervet monkeys use different sounds and calls to warn each other against _____.

Behavioral pattern: Symbiosis, _____, cave dwelling, parasitism are some examples of behavioral adaptations. It is the most _____ adaptation of animals which help in feeding, _____, reproduction.

Name: _____

Date: _____

Try to solve the crossword on "Flightless birds" within 15 minutes.

Across

5. All flightless birds have ___
6. Kiwi is the national symbol of ___
7. Has wings more like flipper and good swimmer
8. Long legged fast runner
13. World's largest penguin
14. Second largest living bird with a beautiful horn like the crest on head

Down

1. covered with tiny hairs
2. species of large bird that can't fly
3. holes in an animal's nose
4. weasel-like animals
5. Kiwi is a ___ bird
9. Birds with a reduced keel or no keel at all on their breastbone
10. In danger of becoming extinct
12. Unusual looking flightless bird which is now extinct
15. This nocturnal flightless bird is the heaviest parrot

05ANIMALS | WS 20

Name: _____

Date: _____

Search for words commonly in context of "flightless birds". Words are placed in all directions (including reverse) and tightly interweaved.

N	I	U	G	N	E	P	R	O	R	E	P	M	E	C	R
M	S	D	V	T	R	F	K	Q	R	H	H	L	O	A	H
C	J	J	T	D	Y	E	E	N	W	P	Q	S	T	T	Q
V	C	W	Y	D	O	D	O	R	V	C	T	I	V	U	B
W	W	B	Z	E	Z	E	S	F	R	R	T	I	M	M	F
Q	S	A	Z	H	W	R	R	J	I	E	J	Q	J	G	H
Q	P	M	U	R	L	E	E	C	S	L	T	S	U	T	B
I	N	K	F	L	I	G	H	T	L	E	S	S	O	J	X
Q	O	M	L	U	W	N	T	O	A	F	E	L	G	K	Z
K	H	Z	Q	V	N	A	A	I	L	V	B	I	O	N	A
W	T	Q	E	D	I	D	E	M	U	C	B	R	S	O	F
W	H	W	U	S	U	N	F	D	O	V	U	T	K	P	D
G	M	I	T	N	G	E	Y	R	A	W	O	S	S	A	C
R	G	W	O	W	N	X	T	B	I	M	H	O	D	K	X
O	Q	C	E	N	E	W	Z	E	A	L	A	N	D	A	A
S	N	L	L	B	P	Z	H	D	L	I	Y	S	L	K	D

FUZZY	EMU	NOSTRILS	FERRETS	FLIGHTLESS	NEW ZEALAND
PENGUIN	Ostrich	RATITES	ENDANGERED	FEATHERS	DODO
EMPEROR PENGUIN	Cassowary	KAKAPO			

29

Name: _____

Date: _____

Do the correct matching.

1	FUZZY -	- covered with tiny hairs	A
2	EMU -	- World's largest penguin	B
3	NOSTRILS -	- Unusual looking flightless bird which is now extinct	C
4	FERRETS -	- Second largest living bird with a beautiful horn like the crest on head	D
5	FLIGHTLESS -	- holes in an animal's nose	E
6	NEW ZEALAND -	- All flightless birds have ___	F
7	PENGUIN -	- Kiwi is the national symbol of ___	G
8	Ostrich -	- In danger of becoming extinct	H
9	RATITES -	- weasel-like animals	I
10	ENDANGERED -	- Kiwi is a ___ bird	J
11	FEATHERS -	- Has wings more like flipper and good swimmer	K
12	DODO -	- Long legged fast runner	L
13	EMPEROR PENGUIN -	- Birds with a reduced keel or no keel at all on their breastbone	M
14	Cassowary -	- species of large bird that can't fly	N
15	KAKAPO -	- This nocturnal flightless bird is the heaviest parrot	O

Name: _____

Date: _____

Search for the words commonly used in the context of "Habitat" in the puzzle. Words are placed in all directions (including reverse) and tightly interweaved.

```
N  T  I  S  L  O  C  Q  N  R  L  O  U  D  X  S
M  O  U  N  T  A  I  N  S  T  M  L  F  E  K  Z
A  D  N  A  P  S  Y  Z  Q  F  M  E  V  N  T  L
R  T  R  F  H  S  E  A  B  E  D  R  M  X  F  S
I  O  W  I  R  H  U  R  A  D  E  S  E  R  T  S
N  P  G  T  N  E  M  N  O  R  I  V  N  E  S  S
E  I  R  L  O  O  S  D  G  F  Y  Q  J  C  F  L
W  X  A  Z  C  S  I  H  Y  E  B  X  J  O  H  S
Y  U  S  S  E  Q  N  S  W  U  S  H  V  S  H  R
Y  Z  S  W  A  B  L  M  L  A  Y  I  F  Y  D  E
C  D  L  A  N  D  H  A  B  I  T  A  T  S  M  V
K  A  A  M  S  D  K  E  T  J  J  E  Q  T  T  I
M  W  N  P  X  E  D  R  V  S  A  G  R  E  K  R
F  Y  D  S  S  O  R  T  A  I  A  G  Z  M  A  Z
V  E  S  I  K  V  M  S  U  B  I  O  M  E  H  Z
C  O  C  L  L  F  F  Y  F  H  A  E  C  Y  X  Y
```

BIOME	ECOSYSTEM	ENVIRONMENT	LAND HABITAT	FORESTS	GRASSLANDS
DESERTS	COASTAL	MOUNTAINS	FRESHWATER	MARINE	LAKES
RIVERS	OCEANS	REEFS	SEA BED	SWAMP	STREAMS

05ANIMALS | WS 23

Name: _____

Date: _____

Unscramble the words which are commonly used in context of HABITATS.

ENVIRONMENT	SEA BED	OCEANS	REEFS	COASTAL	FORESTS
FRESHWATER	LAND HABITAT	MARINE	RIVERS	LAKES	MOUNTAINS
STREAMS	GRASSLANDS	DESERTS	BIOME	ECOSYSTEM	SWAMP

1. **BE MOI**   B _ _ _ _

2. **SO MYCETES**   E _ _ _ _ _ _ _

3. **NON VIREMENT**   E _ _ _ _ _ _ _ _ _ _

4. **TALI HATBAND**   L _ _ _   _ _ _ _ _ _

5. **FOSTERS**   F _ _ _ _ _ _

6. **RGANSDLSAS**   G _ _ _ _ _ _ _ _ _

7. **TRESSED**   D _ _ _ _ _ _

8. **CATALOS**   C _ _ _ _ _ _

9. **OM UNSAINT**   M _ _ _ _ _ _ _ _

10. **HER FRETSAW**   F _ _ _ _ _ _ _ _ _

11. **AIRMEN**   M _ _ _ _ _

12. **LEAKS**   L _ _ _ _

13. **SIR REV**   R _ _ _ _ _

14. **CANOES**   O _ _ _ _ _

15. **FREES**   R _ _ _ _

16. **DEBASE**   S _ _   _ _ _

17. **SAPMW**   S _ _ _ _

18. **MASTERS**   S _ _ _ _ _ _

Name: _____

Date: _____

Fill in the blanks with the words given in the box to complete the passage on "ADAPTATIONS OF MOUNTAIN ANIMALS".

hooves	cold	fur	timberline	inhospitable
lungs	sparse	evolved	climate	perennials
temperature	oxygen	compensate		

Habitats at altitudes are dangerous and _____ than other land habitats. The lives at mountains have to face _____ and other essential gas scarcity; weather is also much harsh in addition to low _____. As the soil is inconsistent, vegetation is also _____ or almost barren. Mountain animals and plants have _____ to make mountains as their habitat; while some are seasonal animals who will migrate according to the weather.

Chamois, ibex, snow leopard, tahr, giant horn sheep are few mountain animals found in mountains. To overcome the bitter _____, they have thick _____ and wool and fast _____ that help them to climb the slopes of the hills. Yaks have large _____ and heart which assist them to _____ the scarcity of oxygen in altitudes. Birds like golden eagle are experts in these regions and for them, it serves as the best place for their breeding and feeding. Trees are thin at heights, but they grow beyond _____ due to climatic conditions. Beyond 3000 feet, at rock zones and snow zones, small grasses, few _____ can be found which can withstand this _____.

Name: _____

Date: _____

Fill in the blanks with the words given in the box to complete the passage on "The world's fastest animal".

flexible	tail	hiding	zebra	adulthood
short	racehorse	smell	endangered	gazelles
eyesight	spotted	cheetah	balance	meal
seconds	camouflage	runner	hyenas	

On the grasslands of Africa lives the world's fastest land animal, the

_____.

What makes this _____ cat such speedy _____? A lean

_____ body and long strong legs that can stretch far forward with

each stride. In fact, a cheetah's stride is as long as a _____. And

while a racehorse might reach speeds of 40 to 45 miles an hour, a cheetah can

burst to a speed of 60 to 70 miles per hour in just a few _____. The

cheetah runs at this incredible speed for only a short distance – the length of a

football field or less. But I sure wouldn't want to be chased by a cheetah, would

you?

That burst of speed is often enough for the cheetah to catch its _____. The

cheetah's running ability is also helped by its long _____ which provides

_____. Cheetahs have good hearing and sense of _____.

However, it's their great _____ that they use for hunting. The

cheetah hunts most often during daylight, including early morning or late

afternoon. When it spots prey it moves in closer under the cover of tall grass.

The cat's yellow-tan, black spotted coat provides _____ in the

grass. The cheetah will get as close as possible to the prey, and then – zoom!

Sometimes the prey is alert and fast enough to escape. When it isn't the

cheetah drags the dinner to a _____ place. A cheetah rests a

_____ time before eating, as the chase is hard work. Sometimes larger and

more powerful predators like lions and leopards, or groups of _____,

steal the food away.

What do cheetahs hunt? Hares, birds and smaller antelopes, like _____ and impalas. They also hunt larger animals like the wildebeest (or gnu) and the _____ when hunting in groups.

Cheetah mothers have an average of three cubs at a time. Cubs have a darker coat, which helps them blend into the shadows when mom goes out to hunt. Still many cubs don't reach _____, with lions, hyenas, leopards and eagles among their predators. Cubs reach full size at around 15 months and stay with their mother for one to two years. Cheetahs once lived in most of Africa and also in parts of Asia. However, much of their habitat and prey has disappeared because of human activity and the cheetah is now an

_____

Answer Sheets

Chapter: Animals

Class 5

05ANIMALS | WS 01

Sort the animals correctly.

Jellyfish	Whale	Squid	Cockroach	Manatee	Dolphin
Sea horse	Shark	Butterfly	Parrot	Hummingbird	Bat
Starfish	Earthworm	Snail	Octopus		

Invertebrates	Vertebrates
Starfish	Sea horse
Octopus	Shark
Snail	Manatee
Butterfly	Dolphin
Jellyfish	Whale
Squid	Hummingbird
Cockroach	Parrot
Earthworm	Bat

OLYMPIAD TESTER

05ANIMALS | WS 02

Fill in the blanks with the words given in the box to complete the passage on "CAMOUFLAGE".

predators	pythons	leaf	savanna	blending
brown	boas	grassy	green	colors
trees	camouflage	spots	trunks	squirrel
marks	pattern	scampering	survival	Prey
African				

In nature, predators and prey seem to play a game of hide and seek. Prey need to hide, so predators do not find them and eat them. Predators need to hide too, so smaller prey cannot see them approaching. Some animals have special colors or marks on their bodies that help them hide among trees, rocks, and grass. This blending is called camouflage.

The earth tone colors of deer and squirrels help them hide from predators among the browns of trees, bushes and soil. A brown squirrel can be difficult to see when it is scampering among brown autumn leaves. A brown deer can be overlooked when it is hiding between tree trunks. The deer and squirrel's special coloring help them hide from predators.

__African__ lions have a tan body coloring. However, lions use it not to hide from predators, but to hide in __savanna__ grasses while watching for prey. A lion can sneak up on prey without being seen more easily by __blending__ into the __grassy__ environment.

Another popular animal camouflage color is green. The green tree frogs of Australia blend in and hide from predators better because of their color. Green tree __pythons__ and emerald __boas__ , meanwhile, are more like lions, using their green color to blend in. When a likely meal (a rodent, bird or lizard) comes along these snakes strike quickly, catching the prey.

The praying mantis takes things a step further. While its __green__ to __brown__ color helps it blend in with vegetation, the mantis also mimics the shape of a stem or __leaf__ . The mantis uses these camouflage methods both to hide from predators like birds, frogs, snakes, spiders and bats, and to await prey such as insects (including other mantises!), spiders, hummingbirds, and small frogs and mice.

Just as important as color camouflage and mimicry is __pattern__ camouflage. Tiger stripes and leopard and jaguar __spots__ are all patterns which help these cats hide among the plants and shadows when they search for prey.

In nature, hide-and-seek is a game of life and death. Pattern and color

camouflage, and mimicry, can give predatorsand prey a survival advantage.

Name: _____

Date: _____

Write the characteristics of birds, fish, mammals, reptiles, and amphibians in this table

	Birds	Fish	Mammals	Reptiles	Amphibians
Covering What type of body covering do animals in this group have? (ex: scales)	feathers	scales	hair or fur	scales	smooth skin
Blood Are animals in this group warm-blooded or coldblooded?	warm-blooded (constant body temp.)	cold-blooded (body temp. changes)	warm-blooded (constant body temp.)	cold-blooded (body temp. changes)	cold-blooded (body temp. changes)
Breathing Do the animals in this group breathe air (lungs) or water (gills)?	lungs (breathe the oxygen in air)	gills (breathe the oxygen in water)	lungs (breathe the oxygen in air)	lungs (breathe the oxygen in air)	both (gills when born; lungs develop later)
Birth Do the young hatch from eggs or are they born alive?	hatch from eggs	hatch from eggs (exception: sharks)	born alive (exceptions: platypus and echidna)	hatch from eggs	hatch from eggs
Milk Do the young drink milk from their mother?	mothers do not feed milk to their young	mothers do not feed milk to their young	mothers do produce milk for their young	mothers do not feed milk to their young	mothers do not feed milk to their young
Backbone Do animals in this group have a skeleton with a backbone?	yes; all vertebrates have a skeleton with a backbone	yes; all vertebrates have a skeleton with a backbone	yes; all vertebrates have a skeleton with a backbone	yes; all vertebrates have a skeleton with a backbone	yes; all vertebrates have a skeleton with a backbone

Fill in the blanks with the words given in the box to complete the passage on "adaptations of an arctic fox ".

scarf	tunnels	bears	camouflage	smell
burrows	fluffy	mammal	rocks	hunter
lemming	northern	paws	hibernate	fat
omnivores	adapted	habitat	energy	

A fascinating hunter makes its home in the Arctic tundra. The fluffy white

 mammal is known to leap high in the air before pouncing on the burrow of its

suspected prey. After a few seconds of furious digging, the small hunter

emerges from the snow-covered ground with a tasty snack, a lemming . What

animal uses such acrobatic hunting techniques? The arctic fox.

Arctic foxes live in all regions of the northern Arctic. You might be surprised

to learn that arctic foxes don't hibernate , even though their habitat is very

cold. They live in underground burrows and are active throughout the year.

These foxes are amazingly adapted for their habitat. Thick multilayered fur

keeps them extra warm. In winter, this coat is white (or occasionally blue-gray).

This provides camouflage in the snow and ice.

In summer, the coat turns a brown-gray, helping the foxes blend in with rocks and small Arctic tundra plants. Arctic foxes have a big fluffy tail. This tail makes a great scarf . Meanwhile, their furry paws, small ears, and short muzzle helps prevent heat loss. The fur on the bottom of their paws keeps them from slipping when they run across ice.

As winter approaches, Arctic foxes increase their body fat by eating as much as they can. This fat provides extra insulation and energy . What do arctic foxes eat? Since these animals are omnivores , they eat other animals (lemmings, hares, small birds, fish, as well as eggs) and plants (berries and seaweed). When food is scarce, they eat the scraps left behind by polar bears and wolves. Arctic foxes can find prey above ground or beneaththe snow because of their excellent senses of hearing and smell .

Arctic foxes usually mate for life. The mother gives birth to five, ten, or even more pups. Both parents raise the pups in underground dens that often include a network of many tunnels .

O5ANIMALS | WS 05

Read the passage below and answer the questions.

What mammal lives only in the Americas, looks a little like a monster-sized pillbug, and wears a coat of armor on its back, head, legs, and tail?

An armadillo, of course.

What is an armadillo's armor like? The armadillo's armor is made up of plates of skin-covered bone. Between these bony sections are flexible bands of skin. Hair grows through the skin on these bands and also on the animal's sides and much softer belly. How many bands an armadillo has depends upon the species.

Where do armadillos live? Wild armadillos live in the grasslands, forests, and deserts of North and South America. One species, the nine-banded armadillo, has extended its range as far north as the United States. They can be found in several states, including Texas, Florida, Georgia, and the Carolinas. Most other species live in South America, with some also in Central America and Mexico.

How big are they? The smallest armadillo, the pink fairy armadillo, is only six inches long. Meanwhile, the giant armadillo can be five feet long and weigh up to 100 pounds. The nine-branded variety that is found in the United States can grow up to two feet long and weigh up to 22 pounds.

Can they roll up in a ball to protect themselves from predators? While the animal's armor provides some protection, only the small three-banded armadillo can roll into a complete ball. Other species escape predators like wild cats and birds of prey by racing into thorny bushes or by burrowing into the ground with their sharp claws. In fact, most armadillos sleep in the warmth of an underground burrow.

What do armadillos eat? Their main diet consists of insects. Using their nose for smelling and their claws for digging, armadillos find beetles, ants and termites and pull them into their mouths with their worm-like tongues. Armadillos also eat plants, fruit, eggs, and small animals, both alive and dead.

What time of day does an armadillo search for food? Well, that depends on the season. Armadillos don't do well in cold weather, so in winter they come out more during the warmth of day. In summer they become more nocturnal, coming out during the night or at dusk or dawn.

Do armadillos swim? You'd think swimming with a suit of armor would be hard. However, by gulping air into their digestive tract armadillos are able to stay afloat as they paddle. Armadillos can also go underwater and walk along a stream bottom for up to six minutes.

Do armadillos live in groups? Armadillos tend to be solitary. However, when it's cold they do sometimes group together.

What are baby armadillos like? At birth an armadillo's armor is soft and leathery. It hardens as the animal grows. Armadillo mothers give birth to differing numbers of young depending upon the species. The nine-banded armadillo always has four identical babies, either four brothers or four sisters.

Are armadillos endangered? The nine-banded variety is not endangered, and their numbers are growing. Most other armadillo varieties are decreasing in number. They've lost habitat to farms and other human settlements. Also, armadillos are often hit by cars while crossing roads. A few people even hunt them for food.

1. An armadillo's diet is mainly composed of _____

   Insects

2. Can armadillos roll up in a ball to protect themselves from predators?

   Only one species of armadillo can roll up into a ball for protection

3. Name two natural predators of armadillos mentioned in the article

   Wild cats and birds

4. Are Armadillos an endangered species

   No

5. An adult armadillo in the United States would probably measure about...

   24 inches long

6. Is armadillo a reptile?

   No. It is a mammal

7. Are armadillos nocturnal?

   Actually, it depends on the season. In winter they come out more during the da
   In summer they become more nocturnal, coming out during the night or at dusl
   or dawn.

8. How big is the group of armadillos?

   Armadillos tend to be solitary. Sometimes during winter, they are see in groups

---

OLYMPIAD TESTER

05ANIMALS | WS 06

Fill in the blanks with the words from the box to complete sentences.

feathers	Turtle	deaf	teeth	Dogs
eagle	Whiskers	echolocation	enemy	friend
fangs	smell	Whale	ears	Insects

1. Mosquitoes can find you by the __smell__ of your body

2. __Dogs__ have an extraordinary sense of smell

3. An __eagle__ can spot it's prey from miles away

4. Dolphins and bats use __echolocation__ for movement

5. __Whiskers__ help the tiger to move in dark and find it's prey

6. Birds do not have __teeth__

7. A snake has two hollow teeth called __fangs__

8. Snakes do not have external __ears__

9. Snake is a/an __friend__ of the farmer

10. Rat is a/an __enemy__ of the farmer

11. Snakes are born __deaf__ . They can only feel vibrations and move with that.

12. __Insects__ are the largest group of animals on Earth

13. __Whale__ is a lung breathing aquatic animal

14. The butterfly has wings but no __feathers__ .

15. __Turtle__ is an aquatic animals that lays eggs on land only

OLYMPIAD TESTER

05ANIMALS | WS 07

Fill in the blanks with the words from the box to complete sentences.

tiny	dolphins	Vertebrates	vertebral_column	octopus
insects	marine	moist_skin	invertebrates	Reptiles

1. Invertebrates are animals that neither possess nor develop a **vertebral column**

2. More than 90% of the animals are **invertebrates**

3. **Vertebrates** are the broad group of animals which are classified by the possession of a backbone or spinal column

4. The **octopus** is considered to be the smartest invertebrates

5. Mammals, Fish, Amphibians, Birds and **Reptiles** are all vertebrates

6. Spiders and **insects** are invertebrates

7. Crabs, prawns, crayfish & lobsters are **marine** vertebates

8. Invertebrates are normally **tiny** and slow moving animals

9. Though **dolphins** and whales are not fish though they live in water and resemble them. They are mammals

10. Frogs breathe through their **moist skin** when they are under water

48

 OLYMPIAD TESTER

Fill in the blanks with the words given in the box to complete the passage on "adaptations in grassland animals ".

water	physical	Organisms	enemies	respond
Behavioral	Structural	habitats	environment	

Adaptation occur in response to changes in the environment , lifestyle, or relationship to other organisms. Organisms that are adapted to their

 habitats are able to secure food and water , obtain spaces, cope with

 physical conditions such as temperature, light, and heat, defend themselves

from their natural enemies , reproduce successfully, respond to changes

around them

There are different types of adaptations:

 Structural Adaptations – These are special body parts of an organism that

helps organisms to survive in its natural habitat. Example: skin colour, shape,

etc.

Physiological Adaptations – These are mechanisms present in an organism that allow it [49] to perform certain biochemical reactions to survive in its natural habitat. Example: ability to produce venom, ability to maintain a constant body temperature, etc.

Behavioral Adaptations – These are ways a particular organism behaves to survive in its natural habitat. Example: being active at night

OLYMPIAD TESTER

05ANIMALS | WS 09

Try to solve the crossword within 10 minutes.

Across

1. forests, grasslands, deserts, coastal and mountain regions
2. Respond to change
3. Have backbones
4. Do not have backbones
7. lakes, ponds, rivers and streams, wetlands, swamp, etc
8. oceans, intertidal zone, reefs, seabed
9. Another name for habitat
11. Fish and Reptiles have ___.
12. Amphibian breathe through this
14. Helps the arctic fox to hide in snow
15. Active at night

Down

5. Live on both land and water
6. natural phenomenon to disguise themselves
10. The movement of organisms in large numbers from one place to another place
13. A smart invertebrate

05ANIMALS | WS 10

Do the correct matching.

1	I	LAND HABITAT	→	forests, grasslands, deserts, coastal and mountain regions
2	B	ADAPTATION	→	Respond to change
3	E	VERTEBRATES	→	Have backbones
4	F	INVERTEBRATES	→	Do not have backbones
5	D	AMPHIBIANS	→	Live on both land and water
6	A	CAMOUFLAGE	→	natural phenomenon to disguise themselves
7	O	FRESHWATER HABITAT	→	lakes, ponds, rivers and streams, wetlands, swamp, etc
8	J	MARINE HABITAT	→	oceans, intertidal zone, reefs, seabed
9	L	BIOME	→	Another name for habitat
10	N	MIGRAION	→	The movement of organisms in large numbers from one place to another place
11	H	SCALES	→	Fish and Reptiles have ___.
12	K	MOIST SKIN	→	Amphibian breathe through this
13	M	Octopus	→	A smart invertebrate
14	C	WHITE FUR	→	Helps the arctic fox to hide in snow
15	G	NOCTURNAL	→	Active at night

OLYMPIAD TESTER

05ANIMALS | WS 11

Search for the words in the puzzle. Words are placed in all directions (including reverse) and tightly interweaved.

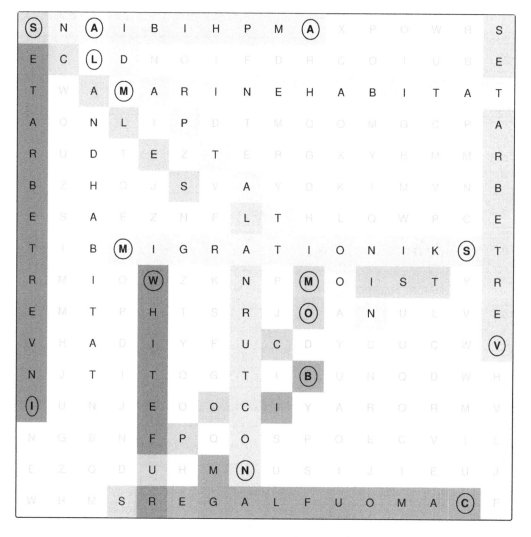

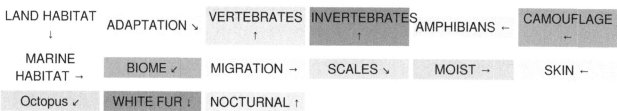

LAND HABITAT ↓   ADAPTATION ↘   VERTEBRATES ↑   INVERTEBRATES ↑   AMPHIBIANS ←   CAMOUFLAGE ←

MARINE HABITAT →   BIOME ↙   MIGRATION →   SCALES ↘   MOIST →   SKIN ←

Octopus ↙   WHITE FUR ↓   NOCTURNAL ↑

15 words in Wordsearch: 5 vertical, 6 horizontal, 4 diagonal. (8 reversed.)

53

 OLYMPIAD
TESTER

ANSWER SHEET

05ANIMALS | WS 12

Unscramble the words

1. htbaaandlt i — L A N D   H A B I T A T

2. ta adaption — A D A P T A T I O N

3. bet traverse — V E R T E B R A T E S

4. vie terebrants — I N V E R T E B R A T E S

5. bi pashmina — A M P H I B I A N S

6. ef glaucoma — C A M O U F L A G E

7. a raibihenmatt — M A R I N E   H A B I T A T

8. be moi — B I O M E

9. it roaming — M I G R A T I O N

10. el sacs — S C A L E S

11. moits — M O I S T

12. kins — S K I N

13. u coopts — O c t o p u s

14. if wuther — W H I T E   F U R

15. no truncal — N O C T U R N A L

54

05ANIMALS | WS 13

ANSWER SHEET

Decode the cryptogram to reveal two amazing animals facts.

A	B	C	D	E	F	G	H	I	J	K	L	M	N	O	P	Q	R	S	T	U	V	W	X	Y	Z
74	67	71	80	68	83	78	85	70	79	76	75	89	82	69	84	77	86	81	87	90	88	72	65	73	66

THE SMALLEST SNAKE IN THE
87 85 68   81 89 74 75 75 68 81 87   81 82 74 76 68   70 82   87 85 68

WORLD IS THE THREAD
72 69 86 75 80   70 81   87 85 68   87 85 86 68 74 80

SNAKE, FOUND IN THE WEST
81 82 74 76 68   83 69 90 82 80   70 82   87 85 68   72 68 81 87

INDIES. WHEN IT IS
70 82 80 70 68 81   72 85 68 82   70 87   70 81

FULL-GROWN IT IS ABOUT
83 90 75 75   78 86 69 72 82   70 87   70 81   74 67 69 90 87

THREE INCHES LONG.
87 85 86 68 68   70 82 71 85 68 81   75 69 82 78

GALAPAGOS TORTOISES ARE
78 74 75 74 84 74 78 69 81   87 69 86 87 69 70 81 68 81   74 86 68

SOME OF THE THE OLDEST
81 69 89 68   69 83   87 85 68   87 85 68   69 75 80 68 81 87

www.olympiadtester.com   54

55

L I V I N G   A N I M A L S   O N   E A R T H .
75 70 88 70 82 78   74 82 70 89 74 75 81   69 82   68 74 86 87 85

O N E   T O R T O I S E   I S   K N O W N   T O
69 82 68   87 69 86 87 69 70 81 68   70 81   76 82 69 72 82   87 69

B E   O V E R   H U N D R E D   A N D   F I F T Y
67 68   69 88 68 86   85 90 82 80 86 68 80   74 82 80   83 70 83 87 73

Y E A R S   O L D .
73 68 74 86 81   69 75 80

05ANIMALS | WS 14

Unscramble the sentences to reveal few amazing animal facts.

1. The heaviest type of snake in the world is the green anaconda. It can grow to

over 300 pounds.

heaviest / of / type / The / snake / grow to over / green / is the /
anaconda. / can / pounds. / 300 / in the world / It

2. A horned lizard can squirt blood out of its eyes when it feels threatened.

threatened. / blood / can / A / squirt / horned / when / it feels / out of
its / lizard / eyes

3. The Komodo dragon is the largest species of lizard on Earth. It has been known

to eat birds, monkeys, goats, deer, and even horses!

largest / of / eat / It / The / and / dragon / even / species / Komodo
/ deer, / to / lizard / on / goats, / has been known / horses! / birds, /
monkeys, / Earth. / is the

4. Some species of snakes can see through their eyelids.

species / of / through / can / their / Some / eyelids. / snakes / see

5. The shell of a turtle has over 60 bones inside of it.

it. / turtle / a / bones / shell / The / 60 / inside / has / of / over /
of

6. _____ _____ _____ _____ _____

_____ _____ _____ _____ _____

_____ _____ _____ _____ _____

_____ _____ _____ _____ _____

_____ _____ _____ _____

their / They / in / bodies / forest. / like / glide / lizards. / birds, /
Southeast / In / there / can / tree / and / to / They / are / flying /
from / fly / don't / exactly / flatten / though. / Asia, / actually / the /
tree

05ANIMALS | WS 15

Unscramble the sentences to reveal few amazing animal facts.

1. Turtles live in every continent except Antarctica.

   live / Antarctica. / in / Turtles / except / every / continent

2. Alligators have about eighty teeth.

   eighty / teeth. / about / Alligators / have

3. Female sea turtles lay up to hundred and fifty eggs at a time. They bury their eggs on a sandy beach and return to the ocean.

   and / beach / bury / up to / to / return / sea / and / at a time. / They / turtles / fifty / Female / lay / ocean. / eggs / sandy / eggs / the / their / on a / hundred

4. When a lizard loses its tail, it can grow a new one.

   a / lizard / can / it / its / When / new / one. / tail, / loses / grow / a

5. Snakes use their tongues to smell their environment.

   to / their / environment. / use / tongues / Snakes / smell / their

6. In Southeast Asia, there are actually flying lizards. They don't fly exactly like birds, though. They can flatten their bodies and glide from tree to tree in the forest.

   their / They / in / bodies / forest. / like / glide / lizards. / birds, / Southeast / In / there / can / tree / and / to / They / are / flying / from / fly / don't / exactly / flatten / though. / Asia, / actually / the / tree

OLYMPIAD TESTER

05ANIMALS | WS 18

Search for 20 INVERTEBRATES in the puzzle. They are placed in all directions (including reverse) and tightly interweaved.

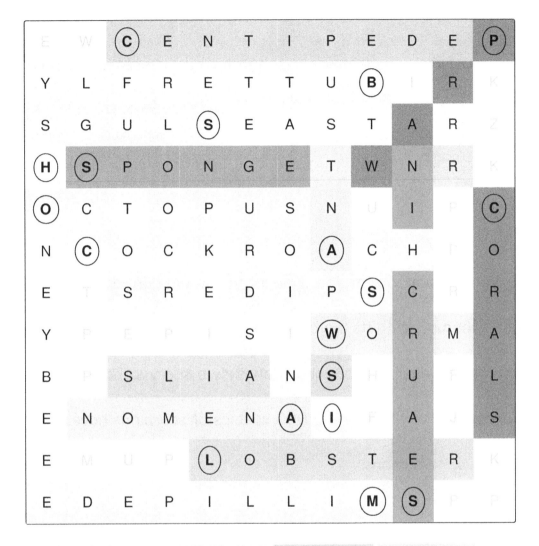

Spiders ←	Insects ↖	Millipede ←	Centipede →	Worm →	Sea star →
Sea urchin ↑	Anemone ←	Corals ↓	Snails ←	Slugs ←	Sponge →
Honeybee ↓	Crab ↖	Prawn ↙	Lobster →	Octopus →	Cockroach →
Butterfly ←	Ant ↑				

20 words in Wordsearch: 4 vertical, 13 horizontal, 3 diagonal. (11 reversed.)

05ANIMALS | WS 17

Fill in the blanks with the words given in the box to complete the passage on "scorpions".

nocturnal	dinosaurs	digestive	eight	predators
insects	inches	tail	consumption	night
caves	dangerous	vibrations	smallest	sight
dangerous	hair-like	feet	venomous	Antarctica
pincers				

If you've ever seen a scorpion, I doubt you would consider it a "cute and cuddly" creature. With its big claw-like **pincers** and its long, curled **tail** and **venomous** stinger, a scorpion is definitely a scary sight. However, only around 30 of the nearly 2,000 species of scorpions have venom considered **dangerous** to humans.

Like spiders and other arachnids, scorpions have **eight** legs and eat meat. They live in deserts, grasslands, forests, and jungles. You can find scorpions on every continent except **Antarctica**.

Scorpions are **nocturnal**, or active during the **night**. They often hide in dark, cool places like leaf litter, burrows, and **caves**. And, yes, they like dark corners in buildings and homes, too. Ancient relatives of scorpions lived before the dinosaurs . Some of these prehistoric scorpion-like creatures grew up to several feet in length. Luckily, today's scorpions are a lot smaller. Most are less than three inches .

You might be surprised to learn that the smallest scorpions are often the most dangerous . Some examples of deadly scorpions are the Indian red scorpion, the Deathstalker of Africa and the Middle East, and the Arizona bark scorpion. Most large species, including the eight-inch African emperor scorpion, are much less dangerous.

Scorpions don't have a good sense of sight . But they do have sensory hair-like structures on their legs and bodies. These structures are capable of feeling vibrations from nearby predators , including tarantulas, centipedes, lizards, owls, bats, shrews, and mice. They can also feel vibrations from their prey, which include a variety of insects , centipedes, spiders, and sometimes, even other scorpions.

Sometimes a scorpion will use its stinger to overcome its prey. All species of scorpions have digestive juices that help soften the scorpion's food, allowing for easy consumption .

05ANIMALS | WS 18

Fill in the blanks with the words given in the box to complete the passage on "ADAPTATIONS".

habitat	withstand	survival	survive	animals
ocean	chameleon	burrowing	color	protection
food	migrate	Antarctica	fat	Grassland
Habitat	hump	reproduction	adaptation	Desert
predators	Tundra	evolution	dominating	climate

 Desert is too hot while Antarctica is too cold for a man to live. But these are habitat for some animals . The property which helps these animals to live in these extreme conditions is called adaptation . Adaptation of animals differs from region to region and according to the climate .

 Habitat is the natural place where animals live. Different organisms prefer the distinct type of conditions and habitat. It may be as big as an ocean or as small as a lake. Some are aquatic while some are terrestrial animals or both. Different types of habitats found on earth are Water, Desert, Forest, Grassland , Tundra and few more. Every animal is native to some region, some migrate from one region to another according to climate.

Adaptation of Animals
When life forms native to an area begin to face some changes in their environment or any threats, either they will die or will adapt for survival . Adaptations are approaches by animals or any organism to live or survive in a specific condition. Every living being is adapted to its habitat. A variety of adaptations can be observed in animals which include behavioral, physiological, anatomical or morphological. The reason for adaptations may be competition for food , weather or for reproduction . As per researchers and scientists, adaptation is the result of evolution over few generations.

Depending on the climate and habitat, animals may show adaptations like changes in color and thickness of skin or fur, shapes of body parts like nose, ears etc. Few types of adaptations are as follow:

Adaptations to extremes: Animals have behavioral and physiological adaptations to withstand the harsh conditions like scarcity of water or oxygen, cold, toxic and corrosive chemicals. For example, hump on a camel for fat storage etc.

Psychological adaptations: Few animals have learning skills like using tools, swimming, emotional behavior like a human. They learn by observation, trials; some mimic others like a chameleon . E.g. Vervet monkeys use different sounds and calls to warn each other against predators .

Behavioral pattern: Symbiosis, burrowing , cave dwelling, parasitism are some examples of behavioral adaptations. It is the most dominating adaptation of animals which help in feeding, protection , reproduction.

05ANIMALS | WS 19

Try to solve the crossword on "Flightless birds" within 15 minutes.

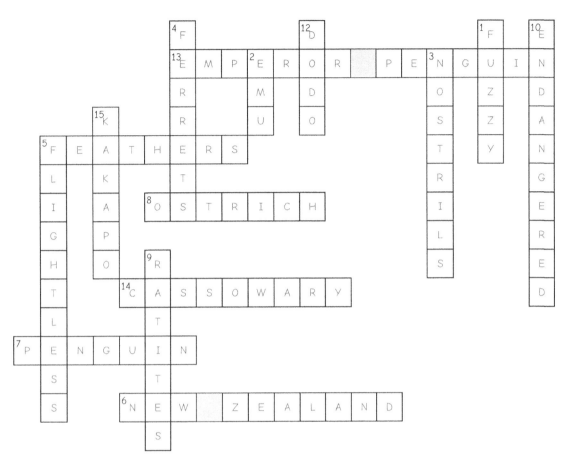

Across

5. All flightless birds have ___
6. Kiwi is the national symbol of ___
7. Has wings more like flipper and good swimmer
8. Long legged fast runner
13. World's largest penguin
14. Second largest living bird with a beautiful horn like the crest on head

Down

1. covered with tiny hairs
2. species of large bird that can't fly
3. holes in an animal's nose
4. weasel-like animals
5. Kiwi is a ___ bird
9. Birds with a reduced keel or no keel at all on their breastbone
10. In danger of becoming extinct
12. Unusual looking flightless bird which is now extinct
15. This nocturnal flightless bird is the heaviest parrot

OLYMPIAD TESTER

05ANIMALS | WS 20

Search for words commonly in context of "flightless birds". Words are placed in all directions (including reverse) and tightly interweaved.

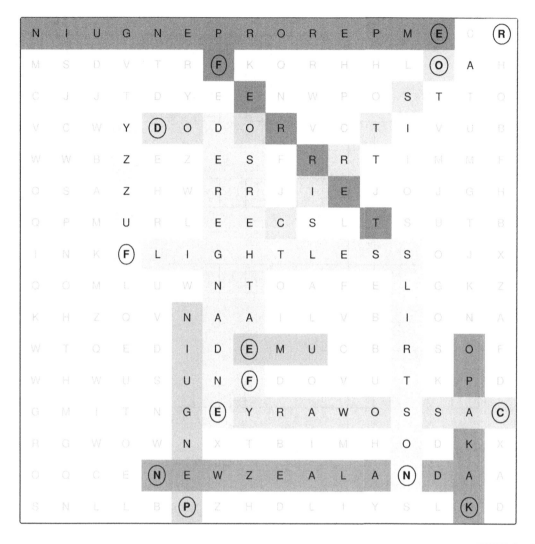

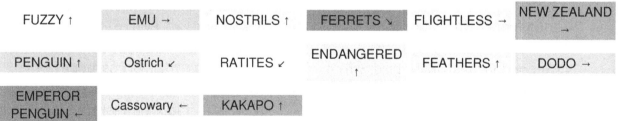

FUZZY ↑   EMU →   NOSTRILS ↑   FERRETS ↘   FLIGHTLESS →   NEW ZEALAND →

PENGUIN ↑   Ostrich ↙   RATITES ↙   ENDANGERED ↑   FEATHERS ↑   DODO →

EMPEROR PENGUIN ←   Cassowary ←   KAKAPO ↑

15 words in Wordsearch: 6 vertical, 6 horizontal, 3 diagonal. (10 reversed.)

05ANIMALS | WS 21

Do the correct matching.

1	A	FUZZY	⇢	covered with tiny hairs
2	N	EMU	⇢	species of large bird that can't fly
3	E	NOSTRILS	⇢	holes in an animal's nose
4	I	FERRETS	⇢	weasel-like animals
5	J	FLIGHTLESS	⇢	Kiwi is a ____ bird
6	G	NEW ZEALAND	⇢	Kiwi is the national symbol of ____
7	K	PENGUIN	⇢	Has wings more like flipper and good swimmer
8	L	Ostrich	⇢	Long legged fast runner
9	M	RATITES	⇢	Birds with a reduced keel or no keel at all on their breastbone
10	H	ENDANGERED	⇢	In danger of becoming extinct
11	F	FEATHERS	⇢	All flightless birds have ____
12	C	DODO	⇢	Unusual looking flightless bird which is now extinct
13	B	EMPEROR PENGUIN	⇢	World's largest penguin
14	D	Cassowary	⇢	Second largest living bird with a beautiful horn like the crest on head
15	O	KAKAPO	⇢	This nocturnal flightless bird is the heaviest parrot

Search for the words commonly used in the context of "Habitat" in the puzzle. Words are placed in all directions (including reverse) and tightly interweaved.

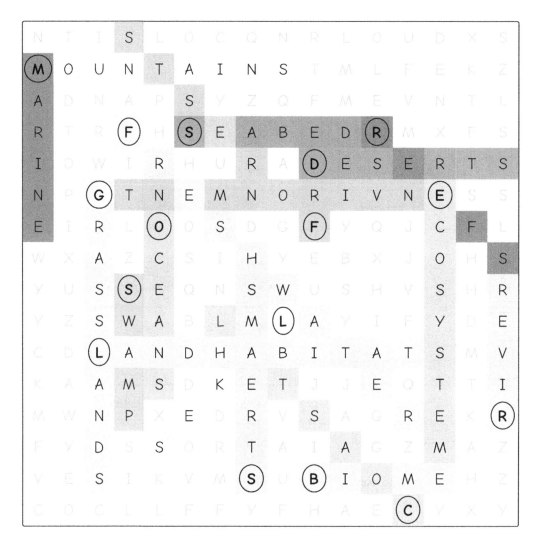

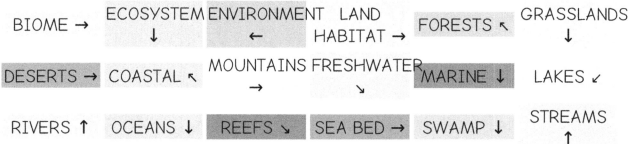

BIOME → ECOSYSTEM ↓ ENVIRONMENT ← LAND HABITAT → FORESTS ↖ GRASSLANDS ↓

DESERTS → COASTAL ↖ MOUNTAINS → FRESHWATER ↘ MARINE ↓ LAKES ↙

RIVERS ↑ OCEANS ↓ REEFS ↘ SEA BED → SWAMP ↓ STREAMS ↑

05ANIMALS | WS 23

Unscramble the words which are commonly used in context of HABITATS.

ENVIRONMENT	SEA BED	OCEANS	REEFS	COASTAL	FORESTS
FRESHWATER	LAND HABITAT	MARINE	RIVERS	LAKES	MOUNTAINS
STREAMS	GRASSLANDS	DESERTS	BIOME	ECOSYSTEM	SWAMP

1. BE MOI   B I O M E

2. SO MYCETES   E C O S Y S T E M

3. NON VIREMENT   E N V I R O N M E N T

4. TALI HATBAND   L A N D   H A B I T A T

5. FOSTERS   F O R E S T S

6. RGANSDLSAS   G R A S S L A N D S

7. TRESSED   D E S E R T S

8. CATALOS   C O A S T A L

9. OM UNSAINT   M O U N T A I N S

10. HER FRETSAW   F R E S H W A T E R

11. AIRMEN   M A R I N E

12. LEAKS   L A K E S

13. SIR REV   R I V E R S

14. CANOES   O C E A N S

15. FREES   R E E F S

16. DEBASE   S E A   B E D

17. SAPMW   S W A M P

18. MASTERS   S T R E A M S

Fill in the blanks with the words given in the box to complete the passage on "ADAPTATIONS OF MOUNTAIN ANIMALS".

hooves	cold	fur	timberline	inhospitable
lungs	sparse	evolved	climate	perennials
temperature	oxygen	compensate		

Habitats at altitudes are dangerous and **inhospitable** than other land habitats. The lives at mountains have to face **oxygen** and other essential gas scarcity; weather is also much harsh in addition to low **temperature** . As the soil is inconsistent, vegetation is also **sparse** or almost barren. Mountain animals and plants have **evolved** to make mountains as their habitat; while some are seasonal animals who will migrate according to the weather.

Chamois, ibex, snow leopard, tahr, giant horn sheep are few mountain animals found in mountains. To overcome the bitter **cold** , they have thick **fur** and wool and fast **hooves** that help them to climb the slopes of the hills. Yaks have large **lungs** and heart which assist them to **compensate** the scarcity of oxygen in altitudes. Birds like golden eagle are experts in these regions and for them, it serves as the best place for their breeding and feeding. Trees are thin at heights, but they grow beyond timberline due to climatic conditions.

Beyond 3000 feet, at rock zones and snow zones, small grasses, few

perennials can be found which can withstand this climate .

What do cheetahs hunt? Hares, birds and smaller antelopes, like _____ and impalas. They also hunt larger animals like the wildebeest (or gnu) and the _____ when hunting in groups.

Cheetah mothers have an average of three cubs at a time. Cubs have a darker coat, which helps them blend into the shadows when mom goes out to hunt. Still many cubs don't reach _____, with lions, hyenas, leopards and eagles among their predators. Cubs reach full size at around 15 months and stay with their mother for one to two years. Cheetahs once lived in most of Africa and also in parts of Asia. However, much of their habitat and prey has disappeared because of human activity and the cheetah is now an

_____

05ANIMALS | WS 25

Fill in the blanks with the words given in the box to complete the passage on "The world's fastest animal".

flexible	tail	hiding	zebra	adulthood
short	racehorse	smell	endangered	gazelles
eyesight	spotted	cheetah	balance	meal
seconds	camouflage	runner	hyenas	

On the grasslands of Africa lives the world's fastest land animal, the cheetah .

What makes this spotted cat such speedy runner ? A lean flexible body and long strong legs that can stretch far forward with each stride. In fact, a cheetah's stride is as long as a racehorse . And while a racehorse might reach speeds of 40 to 45 miles an hour, a cheetah can burst to a speed of 60 to 70 miles per hour in just a few seconds . The cheetah runs at this incredible speed for only a short distance – the length of a football field or less. But I sure wouldn't want to be chased by a cheetah, would you?

That burst of speed is often enough for the cheetah to catch its meal . The cheetah's running ability is also helped by its long tail which provides balance . Cheetahs have good hearing and sense of smell .

However, it's their great eyesight that they use for hunting. The cheetah hunts most often during daylight, including early morning or late afternoon. When it spots prey it moves in closer under the cover of tall grass. The cat's yellow-tan, black spotted coat provides camouflage in the grass. The cheetah will get as close as possible to the prey, and then – zoom!

Sometimes the prey is alert and fast enough to escape. When it isn't the cheetah drags the dinner to a hiding place. A cheetah rests a short time before eating, as the chase is hard work. Sometimes larger and more powerful predators like lions and leopards, or groups of hyenas , steal the food away.

What do cheetahs hunt? Hares, birds and smaller antelopes, like gazelles and impalas. They also hunt larger animals like the wildebeest (or gnu) and the zebra when hunting in groups.

Cheetah mothers have an average of three cubs at a time. Cubs have a darker coat, which helps them blend into the shadows when mom goes out to hunt. Still many cubs don't reach adulthood , with lions, hyenas, leopards and eagles among their predators. Cubs reach full size at around 15 months and stay with their mother for one to two years. Cheetahs once lived in most of Africa and also in parts of Asia. However, much of their habitat and prey has disappeared because of human activity and the cheetah is now an endangered

Made in the USA
Las Vegas, NV
14 August 2024

93787168R00044